D0873912

CAREER PROFILES™

Bill **GATES**

Profile of a Digital Entrepreneur

Brad Lockwood

ROSEN
PUBLISHING®

New York

For the dreamers, inventors, and artists who change the world daily

Published in 2008 by The Rosen Publishing Group, Inc.
29 East 21st Street, New York, NY 10010

Library of Congress Cataloging-in-Publication Data

Lockwood, Brad.
Bill Gates : profile of a digital entrepreneur / Brad Lockwood.
    p. cm. — (Career profiles)
Includes bibliographical references and index.
ISBN-13: 978-1-4042-1906-9
ISBN-10: 1-4042-1906-4
1. Gates, Bill, 1955– 2. Businessmen—United States—Biography. 3. Computer software industry—United States—History. 4. Microsoft Corporation—History. I. Title.
HD9696.63.U62G3742 2008
338.7'6004092—dc22
[B]

2007000020

Manufactured in Malaysia

CONTENTS

INTRODUCTION

There are brief moments when advances in society, industry, and technology create an entirely changed world. The gold rush in the mid-1800s was one, with tens of thousands of Americans racing west to find nuggets in streams, and the oil age was another, with wildcatters from Pennsylvania to Texas digging wells to find black gold. Today's advancement that is changing society is based not on a commodity such as oil or gold, but on technology. The Internet is changing how we live, work, and share our information.

Beginning in the late 1990s, dot-com startups feasting on venture

Directing his tireless ambition to philanthropy, Bill Gates announced that he will leave Microsoft in 2008 to fully focus on the Bill and Melinda Gates Foundation.

capital helped create a new economy based on an electronically connected world. Again, just as they did during the early days of oil or prospecting, many people lost everything while a select few made a fortune.

The computing and Internet age represents the new frontier in creative and technological break-throughs that affect the masses. Emerging in the 1970s, personal computing—leading to the development of the Internet, the World Wide Web, individual Web pages, and finally, blogs—is in part reliant on one man who harnessed technology to forever change the world. Bill Gates is among the most important visionaries of the twentieth century, as well as the richest man in the world due to the appeal of his software creations.

But even though Gates and his company Microsoft have paved the way for the personal computing age, he is criticized as much as he is celebrated. Offering everyone affordable and easy-to-use computers, giving all the world access to powerful educational, business, and communication tools, Microsoft's operating system runs around 95 percent of all personal

Microsoft's sprawling campus in Redmond, Washington, outside of Seattle. It relocated from Albuquerque, New Mexico, in the late 1970s. Other Microsoft campuses are located in India and Ireland.

computers in the world. The company's innovation and dominance are mostly due to Gates's focus and vision. He has always worked for himself, strategically aligning himself and Microsoft to offer the most widely used personal software in the world. Given such domination, Microsoft has also been called a monopoly that undermines alternative technologies and advances. Scott McNealy of Sun Microsystems called Gates "the most dangerous and powerful industrialist of our age."

Opinions of Gates run the gamut, depending on who is asked. Microsoft's partners and most customers praise Gates, while his competitors despise him. His wealth, which also positions him in a league all his own, increases the public's envy and disdain. Gates has been listed in the number-one position on the Forbes 400 list of the wealthiest people in America since 1993. In fact, in an October 1987 issue of *Fortune* magazine, Brian O'Reilly wrote, "Gates apparently has made more money than anyone else his age, ever, in any business."

Perhaps the greatest controversy surrounding Gates stems from confusion about his life. He lives a rather average lifestyle and is an avid reader who plays cards and prefers time with his family versus the spotlight of celebrity. While there is little doubt that he is intellectually brilliant (he scored a near-perfect 1590 on his SAT), in high school Gates was much like many suburban kids today. Born into an affluent family in Seattle, Washington, Gates excelled in math and science, but underperformed in other subjects. He was also eager to play with early computers. Although Gates was once banned from using computers because he was hacking them and was even arrested twice during the same period, his risk-taking methods have proved lucrative. Instead of dropping out of college and becoming a failure, Gates's story is one of luck and fortune. He seized an emerging market and changed an entire industry to create Microsoft. Instead of being a failure and a college dropout, Gates is the world's richest man and one of its most innovative thinkers.

The story of Gates's life is a modern portrait of American success. His life unfolds not in a way that transformed him from rags to riches, but from risky ideas to huge dividends. Although the era of personal computing was barely unfolding, Gates was confident of his vision from the beginning. He was undeterred, and in being so focused, he created new products that forged ways of bringing technology to everyone. Founding an important company and helping to grow a critical industry, Gates is self-created.

His success is due to his own hard work, quick thinking, and maintaining a bold vision of every person using a computer.

Few can criticize Gates for his current passion. He and his wife Melinda are now using his vast wealth to bring education and health care to those who need it most. Armed with more than $80 billion, the Bill and Melinda Gates Foundation is setting its sights on ending HIV/AIDS, polio, illiteracy, and poverty. Gates may be leaving the company he cofounded to help fight the world's problems, but few would bet against his philanthropic endeavors. If his life's story proves anything, it's that a single person with vision, confidence, and creativity can accomplish almost anything.

ONE

CHILD VISIONARY

William (Bill) Henry Gates III was born on October 28, 1955, in Seattle, Washington, the only son of William H. Gates II, a successful Seattle attorney, and Mary Maxwell Gates, a schoolteacher. Bill Gates's parents were both active members of the Seattle community, and Mary Gates was on the board of directors for First Interstate Bank of Seattle, a University of Washington regent, and chairwoman of United Way International, a charity that helps disadvantaged children. Bill has one older sister, Kristianne, and one younger sister, Libby. The Gates family was financially and emotionally

CAREER PROFILES

Seattle, Washington, is the birthplace of Bill Gates. Prior to Microsoft and other technology startups being headquartered in and around the city, Seattle was known for being the headquarters of Boeing Aircraft and, later, Starbucks Coffee.

secure, prominent, and respected in the Seattle area. They had long-standing roots in the Pacific Northwest as William Gates I, Bill Gates's grandfather, was once president of a Seattle bank. From an early age, it seemed that Bill Gates had the ingredients for greatness.

Although many people are blessed with two parents who are educated, wealthy, and supportive, few children will make the impact that Bill Gates has. While he could have pursued any career he wanted and become a successful doctor, lawyer, or banker, instead he imagined an entirely new world and worked to make it a reality. Timing and luck both played a part, but success or failure is often up to the individual, too, no matter his or her background or budget.

Lakeside School

Even during elementary school, Bill showed an attraction toward and an affinity with mathematics. He also enjoyed and had a talent for science. In 1967, at age thirteen, his parents enrolled him in a prestigious and exclusive prep school known as Lakeside, where he was first exposed to computers.

Fate played an early hand in setting Bill on the path to technology. Lakeside School provided students an opportunity to use a variety of early computers, including one where Bill familiarized himself with simple programming languages, a task that excused him from traditional math classes. Bill first taught himself the programming language BASIC. From there, he spent time with another powerful computer, the DEC PDP-10, which was donated to Lakeside by Computer Center Corporation, a local company. Again, Bill made the most of his opportunities, immersing himself in programming and software applications. His mind seemed to be wired for

computer programming. Around this time, Bill was close with childhood friend and neighbor Paul Allen, another Lakeside student who was also interested in computer languages and programming. Bill was only thirteen years old and he was already writing programs for computers. Paul was two years older, but the two were united by their shared interest in technology and innovation. They soon found, hacked, and exploited bugs in the system software of the PDP-10 to gain free computer time, and Computer Center Corporation banned them from using the system altogether. This was Bill's first brush with authority; he later said that he "swore off computers for a year and a half," according to *Blue Magic: The People, the Power and the Politics Behind the IBM Personal Computer*.

First Computer Programs

Still, Bill was hooked. He played the card game bridge and later golf, but his sole hobby and ambition was writing software for computers. In 1968, the company that had banned Bill and his friends, Computer Center Corporation, asked them to help

Founded in 1914 in Seattle, Washington, Lakeside School's prestigious alumni include former Washington governor Booth Gardner, cellular phone innovator Craig McCaw, and television actor Adam West.

find and fix the software problems that they had identified earlier. Getting free unlimited computer time, Bill, Paul, and two other students were able to learn the ins and outs of software, nicknaming themselves "Lakeside Programming Group." At age fourteen, Bill could already feel his life's calling, encouraged by others to use his talents, given access to expensive equipment, and surrounded by other programming enthusiasts. He and Paul would continue to work with and for other computer companies in Seattle, showing early entrepreneurial traits by spending their own money to buy an Intel 8008 processor to write a program, Traf-O-Data, to make traffic counters based on the Intel processor. Although Bill was still in high school, he was already writing advanced computer programs and being well compensated for his work.

Given access to new technologies, Bill and his friend Paul had used their imaginations to create entirely new uses for computers. They were not only getting free computer time, but also earning money ($4,200 for a computer scheduling program for their own school). This is where Bill first displayed his competitiveness and need to be in complete control. During a payroll project for Information Sciences, Inc., a company based in Portland, Oregon, several students wanted Bill to be less involved (thinking the project wasn't big enough for all of them), to which he reportedly said, "Look, if you want me to come back, you have to let me be in charge."

Rethinking their position, the students agreed with Bill, and the project, this time written in the computer language COBOL, was delivered on time. It seems that Bill did not only want to write software, but he also wanted to be in control of every aspect of the fledgling group. This desire for total authority over everything he was involved with would eventually

Bill Gates *(standing)* and fellow student and Microsoft cofounder Paul Allen work on a computer terminal at Lakeside School in 1968.

become one of Bill's traits. This dominant attitude would continue throughout his career. Bill's youth is especially filled with stories like this one where his brilliance and attention to detail remained paramount.

Computers for All

One story about Bill Gates has foreshadowed the impact he would later have in the computer age. Though it has since been repeated many times, it remains anything but fortuitous. During his teens, Gates had a vision that every home would have a computer. Today, the notion does not seem surprising, but in the late 1960s, the idea that everyone would have a personal computer seemed ridiculous. For one thing, computers of that period were huge in comparison to today's models and were not meant to tote from place to place. For another, early computers were affordable only to a fraction of the public. The dream that everyone would one day have his or her own computer was an inspired idea, a notion that only a visionary such as Gates could make a reality.

Technology, however, eventually makes what seems impossible possible. Some of Gates's inspired ideas might be compared to today's students building small businesses on the Web or writing unique software programs for their parents or neighbors. Computing in general allows young minds to explore new possibilities, expand beyond preconceived limitations, and embrace new technologies. Perhaps partly due to his inexperience and lack of awareness of potential limitations, Gates was unafraid of failure.

Gates did what all innovators must: he envisioned an entirely new way of doing things, worked hard, partnered with his peers who had similar interests, perfected his skills, and remained devoted to his dream. Although he was from Seattle, he could have been from anywhere; his parents knew little to nothing about computers or the skills their son was developing as a programmer. But Gates saw the opportunity that computers could provide and he continued to hone his skills as a software developer. Gates wouldn't succeed overnight, but he was already on the cutting edge of new technologies and an entirely new industry. Soon, his interest in computers would lead him down multiple paths with mixed results.

TWO MICROCOMPUTER TO MICROSOFT

By high school, Bill Gates was already successful. He was working for multiple local computer companies and earning more money than most students, but he was also distracted. He was so immersed in computing and so certain of his future success in the industry that he was a mostly average student in all other subjects. Bill had few friends; he limited his social outings to meetings with other computing enthusiasts. Eventually, he became known as a bit of a loner. But Bill wasn't disengaged. In fact, when it came to computer projects, he almost always acted as a manager and leader. Because Bill was balancing

Opened in April 2005, Microsoft's Visitor Center in Redmond, Washington, displays photos of a young Bill Gates *(left)* and Paul Allen. The exhibition also includes early Microsoft products and promotional materials.

schoolwork with a growing software business on the side, however, he did not perform as well in school as he could have.

Bill's parents did what they could to keep their son involved in the community. He served as a page for a state senator and sang in a school music group, but he only wanted to write computer code.

Writing code can be an addictive activity, and creating software offers its authors an incredible feeling of empowerment. Imagine slowly inventing something entirely new such as a software tool or program, and then fine-tuning it until it functions properly, the reward for hours and hours of work. Bill also loved sharing his programming work with good friend Paul Allen, exchanging ideas and using their collective innovation to improve programs even more. Bill was completely fulfilled in his role as a technology innovator. Seeing his ideas emerge on the screen and making the processors perform programs as he instructed them to satisfied him like nothing else could.

Bill had harnessed his creative and mental abilities at a young age and found a method to apply and control them. He wasn't considered the brightest kid in his school, and he certainly didn't have any girlfriends, but he had developed confidence in his programming abilities. His intellect was clearly demonstrated, however, in his SAT scores. Bill scored a nearly perfect 1590. It must be noted that his friend and computing partner, Paul, scored a perfect 1600.

Harvard University

It was time to consider his future. Gates was accepted to Harvard University and began there as a freshman in 1973. At Harvard, Gates majored in computer science and law. His choice of majors combined his interest in computer programming and design with the basics of law. These two subjects would later serve to reinforce Gates's focus on computing as a business. Like childhood friend Paul Allen, Gates would meet a person at Harvard who would figure prominently in his future. Down the hall from him in the dorm was Steve Ballmer, a man who would become critical in their shared success and would eventually replace Gates as CEO of Microsoft some twenty-five years later. Gates's choices of friendships almost seem serendipitous: Gates grew up a few houses away from Paul Allen, and then ended up living only doors down from Steve Ballmer at Harvard. These three would go on to create Microsoft, the most important software company in the world.

Although he was a good student at Harvard, Gates spent every spare moment writing code. In fact, he was so immersed in programming that he hunted for and examined computer code that other students had written. In the 1986 book *Programmers at Work*, author Susan Lammers quotes Gates: "The best way [to be a programmer] is to write programs, and to study great programs that other people have written. In my case, I went to the garbage cans at

the Computer Science Center and fished out listings of their operating system."

However brilliant, Gates was the epitome of a computer geek. He rarely dated or socialized, and he was typically unkempt. His ruffled appearance was often due to the fact that he remained too focused on writing computer code to care about his image, and he almost always surrounded himself with like-minded people. Lacking active social lives, people such as Gates created their own community. Flocking together and sharing new concepts and programs, it didn't matter if he and Ballmer were not popular; they already knew they were on the path to creating software that would change the average person's perception of computers. And although he and Paul Allen attended different colleges (Gates was at Harvard and Allen at Washington State University), they remained close. After two years, Allen dropped out of college to work as a computer programmer for Honeywell in Boston, the same city Gates was in. The trio began working together immediately.

In 1979, Steve Jobs poses with his revolutionary Apple II personal computer, displaying a chess game. Jobs also revolutionized digital media with Apple's phenomenal iPod and iTunes online music service.

The Altair 8800

Perhaps the greatest breakthrough, however, and certainly the most important catalyst for personal computing, came in January 1975, when the cover of *Popular Electronics* magazine bore a mockup of one of the first microcomputers, the Altair 8800. It was designed by Ed Roberts, who started Micro Instrumentation and Telemetry Systems (MITS) to sell model rocket telemetry kits. This new design for a microcomputer astonished and inspired people interested in emerging computer technologies, including Gates and his friends. The Altair 8800 (named for an episode of *Star Trek*) would revolutionize the very concept of computers. Demand for the computer was overwhelming. Roberts had calculated that he would need to sell 200 Altair units to break even, but orders for the $399 kit exceeded 2,000 after its first week on the market.

Allowing the public to buy, assemble, program, and play with an inexpensive computer was an incredible innovation. Every technology hobbyist and

The Altair 8800 microcomputer is shown on display at Microsoft's Visitor Center on April 6, 2005. It was based on the Intel 8080A, one of the first microprocessors.

This 1975 programmer's guide includes a phone number to call for assistance, adding that "...the joint authors of the ALTAIR BASIC interpreter, Bill Gates, Paul Allen and Monte Davidoff will be glad to assist you."

MITS ALTAIR 8800 COMPUTER

early computing enthusiast wanted one, and a young employee at Hewlett Packard named Steve Wozniak would use his Altair 8800 as the basis for another important breakthrough in computing. The first Apple computer was born out of Wozniak's tinkering with the Altair 8800, spawning Apple Computer and the partnership of Wozniak and Steve Jobs. Although the revolution of personal computing had already begun, few had fully realized it. Soon Gates and Allen would jump right in.

Microsoft

It is at this moment that Gates's audacity, diligence, and determination boldly reappeared. Sensing opportunity, and seeing his early vision of every home having a computer in that simple, home-assembled Altair 8800, he didn't hesitate. Apparently out of the blue, Gates called MITS to inform them that he had created a version of BASIC for the Altair 8800. This wasn't true—it is doubtful if Gates or Allen had even used an Altair by that time—but it immediately grabbed the interest of the company. Gates and

Popular Electronics featured the Altair 8800 on the cover of its January 1975 issue, sparking the personal computing revolution. Founded in 1945, the magazine initially focused on amateur radio.

Popular Electronics

WORLD'S LARGEST-SELLING ELECTRONICS MAGAZINE   JANUARY 1975/75¢

PROJECT BREAKTHROUGH!

World's First Minicomputer Kit to Rival Commercial Models...

"ALTAIR 8800"   SAVE OVER $1000

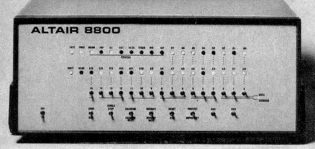

ALSO IN THIS ISSUE:

- **An Under-$90 Scientific Calculator Project**
- **CCD's—TV Camera Tube Successor?**
- **Thyristor-Controlled Photoflashers**

TEST REPORTS:

Technics 200 Speaker System
Pioneer RT-1011 Open-Reel Recorder
Tram Diamond-40 CB AM Transceiver
Edmund Scientific "Kirlian" Photo Kit
Hewlett-Packard 5381 Frequency Counter

Allen were invited to demonstrate their software. Almost overnight, they raced to develop the promised program, both an Altair emulator and the BASIC interpreter, which was a challenge. In a remarkable eight weeks, they succeeded. Just after the demonstration, Gates and Allen were offered a contract deal with MITS to buy the rights to their software. They then formed a company they called Micro-Soft. In late 1975, they dropped the hyphen and just called it Microsoft Corporation, registering the name as a trademark in 1976.

Gates made a bold move and it brought him great success. He wasn't afraid to take risks and he had proven it. Promising to deliver software to a company before he had even created it was unconventional and bold, yet it led to another big decision. After Gates sold his BASIC program under the name Micro-Soft, he decided to end his college career. To the disappointment of his parents, Bill Gates dropped out of Harvard in late 1975, having not finished his junior year but already with a company and contract under his belt. Confident and hopeful, Gates saw his opportunity and took it, too busy writing code to look back.

Few would have made such a fateful leap, especially leaving Harvard to enter an emerging industry, but that's the kind of thinking that separates visionaries from ordinary people. Gates's youth and years of working had come to this important calling, and he seized it. To fully focus on software, his life's quest, Gates left Harvard with no degree to join his childhood friend, another college dropout, Paul Allen, at MITS' headquarters in Albuquerque, New Mexico.

Dropping out of Harvard, the first of many risks Gates would take, would pale in comparison to other decisions he'd soon make. A leap of faith is often required in life, but Gates had left his education behind for a contract with a company that simply couldn't meet demand, would be sold in a short time, and would ultimately go bankrupt.

THREE

LUCKY BREAKS

Few people can say they have worked for only one company during their entire lives, but Bill Gates can. In fact, Gates has always only worked for himself, from doing computer programming for local companies during high school to beginning his own company in 1975. Like many successful people, Gates has followed his vision, even in the face of great risk. Whether quitting college or jobs with other companies, almost all people who make a name for themselves must do it on their own, no matter the challenges or consequences.

Gates moved to Albuquerque, New Mexico, to run Microsoft out of

Microsoft's first headquarters were located in Albuquerque, New Mexico, between 1975 and 1979, as shown on Bill Gates's first business card.

MITS' headquarters in late 1975, just after he had turned twenty years old. He was completely alone, except for the close friendship he shared with his old friend Paul Allen. They were young and successful, and they had their first contract, but Gates's immaturity soon became evident. Before long he was arrested in Albuquerque, once for speeding and another time for driving without a license. However minor these offenses were, they still showed his disregard for authority and rules. Gates was simply unconcerned with anything that was unrelated to technology. Most likely, he was too into his work to even bother with getting or renewing his license, or the thought of doing so simply escaped his mind. He was speeding, both in his car and to create new programs.

Gates's Open Letter to Hobbyists

In addition to his run-ins with the law, yet another facet of Gates's character emerged at this time, one that would help to make his fortune and bring him attention from critics. In February 1976, Gates published "An Open Letter to Hobbyists" that enraged many amateur programmers and foreshadowed his vision for software and intellectual property protection. Claiming in the letter that many users were pirating or using "stolen" copies of the BASIC software that he and Paul Allen had created for the Altair, Gates stated that, without paying for software, the industry and programmers could not afford to produce, distribute, and maintain high-quality products. The future fight over intellectual property rights had begun: Gates demanded payment for his creations while many open-source enthusiasts insisted

Bill Gates's "An Open Letter to Hobbyists," asking users to stop "stealing software," continues to be a major area of debate regarding intellectual copyrights.

February 3, 1976

An Open Letter to Hobbyists

To me, the most critical thing in the hobby market right now is the lack of good software courses, books and software itself. Without good software and an owner who understands programming, a hobby computer is wasted. Will quality software be written for the hobby market?

Almost a year ago, Paul Allen and myself, expecting the hobby market to expand, hired Monte Davidoff and developed Altair BASIC. Though the initial work took only two months, the three of us have spent most of the last year documenting, improving and adding features to BASIC. Now we have 4K, 8K, EXTENDED, ROM and DISK BASIC. The value of the computer time we have used exceeds $40,000.

The feedback we have gotten from the hundreds of people who say they are using BASIC has all been positive. Two surprising things are apparent, however. 1) Most of these "users" never bought BASIC (less than 10% of all Altair owners have bought BASIC), and 2) The amount of royalties we have received from sales to hobbyists makes the time spent of Altair BASIC worth less than $2 an hour.

Why is this? As the majority of hobbyists must be aware, most of you steal your software. Hardware must be paid for, but software is something to share. Who cares if the people who worked on it get paid?

Is this fair? One thing you don't do by stealing software is get back at MITS for some problem you may have had. MITS doesn't make money selling software. The royalty paid to us, the manual, the tape and the overhead make it a break-even operation. One thing you do do is prevent good software from being written. Who can afford to do professional work for nothing? What hobbyist can put 3-man years into programming, finding all bugs, documenting his product and distribute for free? The fact is, no one besides us has invested a lot of money in hobby software. We have written 6800 BASIC, and are writing 8080 APL and 6800 APL, but there is very little incentive to make this software available to hobbyists. Most directly, the thing you do is theft.

What about the guys who re-sell Altair BASIC, aren't they making money on hobby software? Yes, but those who have been reported to us may lose in the end. They are the ones who give hobbyists a bad name, and should be kicked out of any club meeting they show up at.

I would appreciate letters from any one who wants to pay up, or has a suggestion or comment. Just write me at 1180 Alvarado SE, #114, Albuquerque, New Mexico, 87108. Nothing would please me more than being able to hire ten programmers and deluge the hobby market with good software.

Bill Gates

Bill Gates
General Partner, Micro-Soft

that all code should be free to use and be adapted by others.

This is a major point of contention for most computer enthusiasts and programmers: Microsoft's source code has always remained "closed" (securely encrypted so no outsider may view or alter it), while other source code (including early Altair programs and today's Linux) remains "open." Using copyrights and lawsuits to protect his creations was clearly important to Gates three decades ago, and certainly remains so today. It takes hours, even weeks and months, to write effective programs that function properly. For this work, Gates demanded that his software creations remain under his control. It seems like a simple demand, but complex computing involves multiple programs working together, in tandem. Understandably, other developers wanted access to the code, which Gates continually kept secret and protected through all means. From his "Open Letter to Hobbyists" in 1976 to today, Gates and Microsoft have fended off other programmers who have tried to use or adapt their source code. Early on in the computing era, this was an unconventional and controversial concept.

Again, Gates's timing was both fortunate and strategic. By the late 1970s, the personal computing market was slowly warming up. MITS couldn't keep up with demand for its Altair, and other manufacturers such as Atari, Commodore, Amiga, and Apple were emerging to serve the ever-growing market.

Increased competition and poor business decisions hurt MITS; nearly 10,000 Altair 8800s were eventually sold, but so, too, was the company in 1977, eventually going bankrupt and becoming a footnote in the history of computers. The industry was expanding at an alarming rate, but its companies were in a state of disarray, including Microsoft. Gates's fledgling business was on the verge of losing its first major contract to a company that would soon be out of business.

Forging Ahead

Already Gates was interested in diversifying and expanding his business, always searching for new customers for Microsoft's BASIC software. In doing so, Microsoft opened its first international offices in Japan (ASCII Microsoft, now known as Microsoft Japan) in 1979. Gates also moved Microsoft's headquarters from Albuquerque to Bellevue, Washington, which was closer to where both Gates and Allen grew up. Steve Ballmer, Gates's friend from Harvard, joined the company in 1980, and Microsoft Inc. was officially registered in the state of Washington, with Gates as president and chairman of the board, and Allen as executive vice president.

Now an official corporation with employees, Microsoft and its founders were busy adapting a variant of UNIX (the major operating system at the time) in 1980. Contradicting Gates's insistence on protecting intellectual property, Microsoft had actually acquired the original code in a licensing deal with AT&T and was slowly releasing its adaptation publicly. The product, first dubbed Xenix, would become Microsoft's first and still highly popular word processor, MSWord. Again, Gates was contradicting himself. Although he had fiercely insisted on protecting his own creations (and made his opinions known in his "Open Letter to Hobbyists" in 1976), he still didn't appear fully opposed to coopting or relicensing others people's creations. This is a trend in Gates's career, and it becomes most clear during a critical moment of his life—Microsoft's lucky break.

International Business Machines

International Business Machines Corporation (IBM), then known by some computer enthusiasts as "Big Blue," was ready to enter the personal computer market. The behemoth of business computing, IBM brought massive investment and credibility to personal computing. Seeking to tap into the growing demand, IBM immediately needed partners for the new initiative. This was a rapid launch for such a large company and secrecy was at the forefront. Among industry rumors was the belief that the only reason Microsoft got the IBM contract is because Gates signed IBM's non-disclosure agreement without question. Other companies, Microsoft's competitors included, balked and wanted to take more time,

Paul Allen and Bill Gates are shown in 1981 on the verge of licensing Microsoft's operating system (which Microsoft had licensed from others) to the computing giant IBM.

but Gates saw the opportunity to work with IBM and didn't hesitate.

Initially, Gates and Allen wanted to get the contract to deliver BASIC for the new IBM PC, like they had for the Altair. In an ironic twist, Gates actually sent IBM to a competitor, Digital Research, for the operating system, but when negotiations stalled (Digital Research delayed reviewing the terms of the non-disclosure agreement) IBM came back to Microsoft. Once again, Gates's decision-making skills that embraced risk proved timely. And again, he promised what he didn't actually have in his possession.

But another person did. Tim Paterson of Seattle Computer Products had written what he called "Quick and Dirty Operating System" (QDOS), and Allen led the effort to obtain it. Accounts of the story vary, but if Paterson had known that his QDOS was intended for IBM, he may have refused—or at least asked for more money. For less than $100,000 (rumored to have been closer to $50,000), Microsoft purchased Paterson's operating system and adapted it. Within months, Microsoft provided IBM with its operating system, renamed PC-DOS, in late 1981.

DOS quickly became the cornerstone for Microsoft's emerging success. The company now had an operating system as well as a major partner in IBM. Highly adaptable and aggressive, maybe even misleading at times, Gates and Allen had once again gotten a contract by promising what they didn't have. Whether for the MITS Altair or the IBM PC, Gates's and Allen's eagerness for success spurred them to locate and capitalize on their opportunities by adapting someone else's computer code. The purchase and adaptation of Paterson's QDOS had made Microsoft the key software supplier in the personal computer industry. Although the industry is based on innovation, Gates had an early knack for eliminating any competition, making Microsoft an industry leader from the beginning.

Microsoft Dominates the Market

Supported by a massive marketing campaign, the IBM PC was a huge success. Although it was more expensive than other personal computers at the time, selling for $2,880 in 1981, the masses trusted the IBM name. More important, especially for Microsoft, the IBM PC had been built with "off the shelf" components, meaning that other manufacturers were soon shipping their own "clones" of the IBM PC. Sensing the potential of tapping into this expanding demand, Gates and Allen quickly converted PC-DOS,

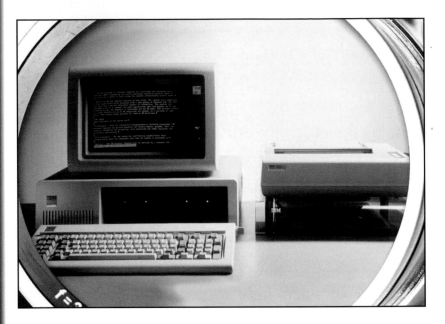

Launched on August 12, 1981, the IBM 5150 PC changed how people and businesses use computers. It was discontinued on April 2, 1987.

which they had licensed to IBM, to MS-DOS in order to supply the other manufacturers making clones of the IBM PC. Many look at this as a major misstep for IBM—allowing Microsoft to relicense its software to other competing clones—but it certainly shows how quick Gates and Allen were to take advantage of their unique position, based mostly on an operating system actually developed by someone else.

Soon the world was overwhelmed with personal computer clones that were manufactured to be like

IBM's personal computer. All of them were running the software that Gates and Allen licensed from Paterson, then adapted for PCs. IBM may have given Microsoft a lucrative contract, but the company was quick to sign deals with other companies to resell its wares. Whether an IBM, Compaq, or later Dell or Hewlett Packard, if it was an IBM PC clone, it was running a version of the Microsoft operating system, and each manufacturer was paying licensing fees to Microsoft.

Microsoft's business model was ideal. Write the programs once and then sell them over and over, reaping in the profits. Although programming takes many people hundreds, if not thousands, of hours to write and compile code that functions properly, once completed it can be sold innumerable times. Microsoft was now supplying multiple manufacturers, reselling the same software it had written for IBM, and feeding the personal computing frenzy. What had begun with hobbyists and fellow geeks playing on the Altair 8800 had become big business. Personal computing didn't even exist when Gates and Allen started writing code and hacking in high school, but they were heading the company that was in the center of an entirely new craze.

On His Own

Tragically, the successful partnership at Microsoft would end suddenly. In 1983, Allen was diagnosed with Hodgkin's disease and forced to resign from Microsoft for medical treatment. He made a full recovery, but he never returned to full-time work at the company he'd started with Gates only eight years earlier. Allen would remain on the board of directors of Microsoft, but his focus instead became investing in other technology, entertainment, and professional

Microsoft's Visitor Center exhibits a cut-out display of the company's eleven employees in 1978. Excluding Bill Gates, each former employee's 2006 worth ranges from $2 million to $22 billion.

sports teams. Eventually, he would own a cable company, the Portland Trailblazers, and the Seattle Seahawks. His importance to the early founding and success of Microsoft cannot be understated, but it was now up to Gates to carry the company forward.

Through good timing, risk, business savvy, and a little luck, Microsoft had cornered the emerging personal computing industry. But Gates was now alone and growing concerned about how he was going to lead a team of young programmers forward. His goal was to focus Microsoft on writing both operating systems and applications, and he continued to write code as well while trying to manage business tasks. Gates's college friend Steve Ballmer took over much of the management and marketing for Microsoft, a rather demanding job due to the fact that Microsoft software was now a part of nearly every personal computer on the market. As a result, Gates was becoming rich, and even famous, appearing on the cover of *Time* magazine for the first time in 1984. But even he could not have envisioned what was on the horizon.

Another company also founded by two friends would soon release a breakthrough in personal computing, called the Macintosh. Soon Microsoft's Windows system would rewrite the way we use

APRIL 16, 1984

$1.75

TIME

COMPUTER SOFTWARE
The Magic Inside the Machine

**Microsoft
Boss
Bill Gates**

On April 16, 1984, Bill Gates first appeared on the cover of *Time*. The magazine would go on to name him one of the 100 most influential people of 2004, 2005, and 2006.

computers and the way in which people viewed computer geeks such as Gates. Once hailed and lauded, Gates would eventually become demonized and scorned. His software innovations would come back to haunt him, and Microsoft's dominance over personal computing would soon be seen as a detriment to the industry at large.

FOUR

WINDOWS TO THE WORLD

The early 1980s were a period of great change in Bill Gates's life, career, and company. Winning the lucrative operating system and software license for IBM PCs, then promptly losing his day-to-day relationship with childhood friend and partner Paul Allen, became the very definition of a company going through growing pains. Little did Gates know that his life and career were about to face some serious personal and financial challenges.

In 1985, Gates sent a rather remarkable memo to the management of Apple Computer. Prophetic and provocative, Gates first praised the new Apple Macintosh computer's design, then denounced it as a failure because it did not follow the IBM PC clone strategy. The future was licensing software to many companies, Gates boldly asserted; selling add-ons for computers, like graphics cards and other hardware items, was the way to increase market share and profits. Why shouldn't Apple use a similar business model as Microsoft? As bold as it was brash, Gates's memo closed by saying that if Apple didn't license its operating system to other computer companies, it would not become a second standard to the IBM PC clones. Gates was essentially claiming that Apple would fail as a company if it did not follow the same path that Microsoft had created. For obvious yet questionable reasons, Apple Computer ignored the memo. But, by then, the company could hardly ignore its author.

Apple vs. Microsoft

From the beginning, few people claimed that Microsoft offered the world's best software products. They frequently contained bugs (hidden errors), crashed too often, and were generally considered too unstable and insecure for mission-critical applications such as military and corporate computing. In short, Microsoft's products have always been a bit

temperamental. One reason for the inaccuracy could have been because the systems were based on another operating system and were actually multiple programs pieced together. Critics of Microsoft have often claimed the company typically focused more on offering new products than on making sure each product worked perfectly. Microsoft is sometimes considered the opposite of Apple, a company that has earned a cult-like following because of its record of innovation, stability, and creativity.

However, Microsoft's business model, coupled with massive marketing and support from major industry partners/licensees including IBM, was indeed the path to larger market shares and profits. The memo was correct; Gates was seeing the future. Despite its fine products, Apple's resistance to licensing its operating system to other manufacturers would limit its long-term growth as a company. The Macintosh may have been the superior personal computer at the time, especially when compared to the many PC clones, but Microsoft's name recognition and revenues were growing exponentially. Marketing

In 1985, Bill Gates poses with a floppy disk of Windows 1.0, a 16-bit operating system. It was released on November 20 of that year.

and partnering were now as essential as innovation and quality in order to remain on top of the personal computer industry.

The similarities and differences between Apple Computer and Microsoft are incredibly revealing. Both companies were founded by two men, and both would soon lose a cofounder early: Paul Allen at Microsoft and Steve Wozniak at Apple. Allen and Wozniak would move on, leaving behind the companies they helped launch, and leaving their former partners alone to confront the massive growth of

Steve Jobs *(left)* of Apple Computer debuts the new Macintosh in California on February 6, 1984. He and Steve Wozniak built the first Apple computer in 1976.

the industry. However, once alone, Gates and Steve Jobs would take their companies in opposite directions, yet both paths were fueled by the same basic concept: the user-friendly graphical user interface, or GUI.

Gates admitted that the Macintosh computer was indeed a breakthrough. Its GUI, which used a mouse to click on icons and ease complex computing instructions with a single touch, was extremely user-friendly. Finally, anyone who had never before used a computer could understand how with little effort. (Interestingly, Xerox had first developed the user-friendly GUI and mouse, but never took it to market.) The new Macintosh was indeed a marvel, and in it Gates saw both the future and another way to take advantage of his market position. Development for what Gates called "Windows" was announced as early as 1983, but progress was slow, to Apple's benefit.

Gates and Windows

By 1984, seven million personal computers had already been sold, making Microsoft a top-earning company in the United States. The new Macintosh hit the market with great fanfare, and it sold rapidly to artists, designers, and educators eager to buy and

Bill Gates lies on his desk during a brief moment of downtime after the launch of Windows 1.0 in 1985.

use the easy-to-operate and innovative computer from Apple. But the Macintosh system was also more expensive, so cheaper clone PCs running Microsoft operating systems still gained in overall market share. Larger, more efficient companies entering the personal computer market (based on IBM's PC and Microsoft's DOS operating system) gave the industry a momentum that couldn't be stopped.

By 1986, more than 50 percent of all personal computers were PCs; by 1987, six million of nine million were PCs. Even today, when people mention personal computers, they invariably think of those running Microsoft software. Of the many early personal computer manufacturers, only Apple remains. Most would fail due to poor management (like MITS and the Altair), or because they simply couldn't compete against larger rivals running Microsoft (like Atari and Commodore).

The success of the IBM PC and its clones virtually made Microsoft into a mega company and earned Gates millions of dollars. On March 13, 1986, Microsoft went public with its stock; its initial public offering (IPO) per share of stock was $21.00. As a result, on that day, Gates became an instant millionaire. Although he was only thirty-one years old, he was quickly becoming one of the wealthiest men in the United States. But these earnings were only the beginning. For every PC sold, Microsoft received licensing fees and sold add-on programs, steadily increasing its market share and stock value.

By 1990, PCs were owned by 84 percent of computer users (or about sixteen million people), then selling millions more than the 1.3 million Macintoshes that were sold that same year. Although

Apple was increasing its sales, the total personal computer market was growing so rapidly that the company was actually losing market share to PCs. With the release of Windows 3 in 1990, then 3.1 in 1991, Microsoft became the leader in providing PCs for small businesses, mid-sized companies, and even education, a sector once almost exclusively loyal to Apple.

Bill Gates's predictions had come true. The Macintosh may have been the better computer, but Apple couldn't compete with inexpensive PC clones that ran Microsoft applications. Apple's market share peaked at 12 percent in 1993, and even Microsoft's former partner IBM was starting to see Gates's company as a threat. One year earlier in 1992, IBM released OS/2 2.0, an attempt to challenge Microsoft's position with Windows. OS/2 2.2 had brief success, but even mighty IBM, like Apple and so many other companies, ceded to Gates's winning software strategy of licensing to multiple manufacturers.

Easily, this period marked the most exciting and successful time of Gates's life. In 1992, President George H. W. Bush honored Gates with the Medal of Technology for his many accomplishments. Then, in 1993, *Fortune* magazine declared Microsoft the "Most Innovative Company Operating in the United

States." It was during that same year that Gates also appeared on the Forbes 400 list as the wealthiest man in America. Ending the year on the highest of notes, on New Year's Day, 1994, something even more remarkable took place: Bill Gates married Melinda French, a marketing manager at Microsoft. Originally from Dallas, Texas, French won Gates's heart, and the two would have three children, Jennifer Katherine Gates (in 1996), Rory John Gates (in 1999), and Phoebe Adele Gates (in 2002). It seemed amazing that a man so focused on technology—a self-professed technology geek—would find time for love, especially at the relatively late age of thirty-eight. Suddenly, however, and thanks in large part to Gates's tremendous success and his embrace of the major news media outlets, being a technology geek was no longer such a bad thing.

Start Me Up

The personal computing revolution had begun. There was a new confidence, as well as a new means of communication, spreading throughout America and the world. New technology and the booming computer industry were creating high-paying jobs, and anyone with technology experience was in demand. Use of the Internet, originally developed by the

American military in the late 1950s, and the World Wide Web was spreading, creating new companies and incredible wealth. People such as Gates, once ignored or outright ridiculed, were suddenly driving a new information economy. The Internet Age was in full swing.

Microsoft's Windows 95 software was launched with incredible spectacle and excitement. A huge advertising campaign was launched that featured the Rolling Stones' song "Start Me Up" as its theme, showing people of all ages tapping into the new computer and information revolution. Gates accepted his role as a celebrity amid the fanfare, proudly demonstrating his company's new offering and doing more public speeches and interviews. The new user-friendly operating system from Microsoft cemented its position and pushed the company to even greater heights. Windows 95 incorporated multiple existing features, including long filenames and preemptive multitasking, but repackaged and rebranded as "new." The response was astonishing. Software developers started to partner and program ancillary packages

Midnight on August 24, 1995, Mikol Furneaux seizes two boxes of Windows 95 in Sydney, Australia. Microsoft anticipated selling 30 million copies worldwide by year's end.

for Microsoft, and clients appreciated the slick and user-friendly design. This was the death knell for IBM's OS/2, as well as Apple, with sales reaching an all-time high of 4.5 million units, then plummeting soon after. Meanwhile, total PC sales were approaching 100 million. There seemed to be no stopping Microsoft.

The success of Microsoft had allowed Gates to create a dynasty. He had acquired great wealth and notoriety, a position that he gladly shared with stockholders and employees. As a result of the astonishing success of Microsoft, its stock price had increased 100-fold since 1986. Anyone who bought Microsoft stock when it was first offered was now rich. A modest $10,000 investment in Microsoft in 1986 was worth $1,000,000 only a decade later! More striking is the fact that in 1986, there were already around 10,000 "Microsoft Millionaires." Programmers, managers, and even secretaries working at Microsoft were suddenly wealthy. Gates's employees were swimming in cash. Their faith, hard work, and stock in the company had paid enormous dividends, literally.

Such wealth altered the entire Pacific Northwest region. Seattle was quickly becoming known as a proving ground for technology innovation. Gates's employees working on the sprawling Microsoft campus in nearby Redmond, Washington, were spending their newfound wealth in the local community, and his former partner Paul Allen had also invested in new companies in the region. Silicon Valley, the area around San Francisco, California, was also experiencing a technology renaissance during the same time. Seattle's economy was booming as well. Even when the city's biggest employer, Boeing, moved its headquarters years later, the economy remained robust. It now had technology and a

While Microsoft is headquartered to the north in Washington State, northern California's Silicon Valley is home to Yahoo!, Google, and many other technology giants.

growing coffee company, Starbucks, to stabilize its wealth, jobs, and image.

Innovator or Procrastinator?

The future seemed bright, especially for Microsoft, a company created on new ideas. The only remaining question was how large could Microsoft expand? With more than a 90 percent market share, billions in revenues, and an increasing number of employees, it seemed that the only thing that could possibly threaten Microsoft's dominance was a better idea. Like Apple and other innovators, would Microsoft remain on top, or would something stop the company's growth? Remarkably, there were several obstructions that were brewing while Microsoft was enjoying its period of mega success. Soon a variety of those factors would combine to give Gates and Microsoft its greatest challenge.

By the mid-1990s, Gates was no longer writing code. He was instead running Microsoft, now a major corporation with tens of thousands of employees and millions of customers. But the emerging Internet was rewriting the rules of computing and business, and it was quickly becoming a tremendous threat to his company's position. Startup companies such as Netscape were changing the way people used their computers, offering browsers to search the Internet and World Wide Web, while others were raising millions of dollars from investors for the next great idea. Suddenly, people everywhere seemed to set their eyes on Microsoft for the next big technological innovation.

It was the Internet that fully exposed the flaws in Microsoft's software products. From stability to security, the many versions of software that Gates had cobbled together and revised over the years were now vulnerable to hackers and competitors. Viruses, "worms," and "Trojan Horses" were being created en masse to exploit holes in Microsoft's software. It is ironic that Gates got his start (his first job and free computing time) by exposing weaknesses in other software brands, and now his own company was being criticized and attacked for the same. According to Steve Ballmer, Gates was the most spammed person in the world during this period. He received more than four million e-mails each day. It seemed, due to Microsoft's position and problems with its products, hackers, spammers, and virus writers were targeting both Gates and his company.

For a time it seemed that only people who were not running Windows were immune to hackers and viruses. Even worse, Microsoft seemed to have no

BILL GATES

THE
ROAD
AHEAD

COMPANION
INTERACTIVE
CD-ROM
INSIDE

plan to create a browser so that its customers would have companion software to use the Internet. It seemed astonishing that the most important software company in the world appeared unprepared for the advent of the World Wide Web. It was also ironic because in 1995, Gates's book *The Road Ahead* offered his vision for the future of computing, even as millions of people using computers running Microsoft software were getting online for the first time. Years later, Gates admitted that his hesitation to anticipate how important the Internet would become was a huge oversight. In a 1998 speech at the University of Washington, he said, "Sometimes we do get taken by surprise. For example, when the Internet came along, we had it as a fifth or sixth priority."

Open vs. Closed Systems

Such sudden access to alternative ideas, as well as new technologies, made the Internet a major area of vulnerability for Microsoft. The "platform independence" of the Internet (meaning that anyone using

The first of many best-selling books by Bill Gates, *The Road Ahead* was released on November 18, 1995, to both rave reviews and harsh criticism.

any computer could access HTML-based Web sites)
made Gates's products appear highly proprietary,
restrictive, outdated, and even obsolete. Why use a
"closed" Microsoft PC when the Internet is completely
open and accessible? Other customers wondered if
they should use Microsoft at all, since it required
expensive and unstable add-ons when so many alternative technologies were suddenly becoming available.

This development points to yet another problem
in Gates's overall strategy. For more than two
decades he had been protecting the source code for
his software, but the Internet was at last allowing programmers to share tools, code, and information to
create more stable and secure programs. Linux, an
"open-source" concept in programming, was suddenly gaining popularity and threatening to steal
part of Microsoft's market share. Linux was less
expensive than Microsoft, as well as more adaptable.
Programmers from all over the world were developing
upgrades, alternative programs, and tools with Linux,
and the importance of open-source software was
being realized. Companies and countries were interested in Linux and other open applications, hoping
to cut the expense of Microsoft's many upgrades.

With thousands of open-source developers
building new applications, and billions of dollars

being invested into Internet startups, it seemed that the biggest loser would be Microsoft. Other Internet-based applications and competitors were on the rise; Microsoft's own Internet supplier, Microsoft Network (MSN), was not catching on as quickly as expected. Gates and Microsoft were at odds. Talented Microsoft employees were leaving for other lucrative offers and its stock price was becoming stagnant. In fact, Microsoft's past success was now being over-shadowed by sudden startup success stories such as eBay and Yahoo!.

For the first time, Microsoft was highly vulnerable with the increased emergence of criticism, hackers, and viruses. Gates, who wrote in his book *The Road Ahead*, "Success is a lousy teacher [because] it seduces smart people into thinking they can't lose," was being tested.

Increased Diversity

Instead of focusing on improving Microsoft's software security, Gates denied there was a problem. In October 1995, he was quoted in *Focus* magazine as saying, "There are no significant bugs in our released software that any significant number of users want fixed." Microsoft was partnering with NBC to create a 24/7-cable news service, MSNBC, in 1996, rather

On July 15, 1996, Bill Gates appears on a large-screen TV for a press conference to promote the launch of the twenty-four-hour NBC Microsoft television news channel MSNBC.

than focusing its energies on creating new Internet-based technologies or improving its software security.

In addition, Microsoft had made it a priority to launch Windows CE, operating software for palm (hand-held) computers. The response to the release was mixed. More focused on controlling content and inventing futuristic toys than making current products more secure, Microsoft and Gates seemed to be courting disaster. Instead of innovating, Microsoft was buying. Reports at the time stated that one of the company's biggest problems wasn't making money, but managing all of the money it already had (more that $18 billion, according to one report). Using its clout and cash, the company invested in other startups and even its former nemesis, Apple, which only furthered criticism from diehard PC users. Many people wondered how Apple could compete against Microsoft when it was partly owned by Microsoft.

The company may have more than $30 billion in annual revenues, and its president is the richest man on Earth, but they were starting to be seen by many as the "old guard" compared to the Internet's eager upstarts. Investing in others and controlling its position, the most influential software company in the world seemed to be sitting on the sidelines during the Internet craze. Microsoft was viewed as an unfocused latecomer that was playing catch-up. Another book by Gates, *Business @ the Speed of Thought*, was released in 1999, became a best seller, and was translated into twenty-five languages. But the world was changing so rapidly, many speculated that Gates and his company were being left behind.

Trouble Ahead

Sales of personal computers remained strong, especially due to another trend that was hitting the

Bill Gates signs copies of his second book, *Business @ the Speed of Thought*, at a bookstore at the London Business School on March 26, 1999.

marketplace. Incredibly inexpensive computers were becoming available, remarkably for well under $1,000. Since most of them were running Microsoft's operating system and applications, this trend pointed to the need for less expensive software. The concept of "network computing" was only exacerbating this trend. Many competitors, including Oracle and Linux, were promoting stripped-down computers (as opposed to Microsoft's bulky installations) to allow users access to the Internet and company servers without needing all of the software that Microsoft required for each machine. People began wondering why they needed such expensive software when hardware itself was becoming more inexpensive. With computer hardware prices plummeting, and each Microsoft installation staying at around $100, the only one that seemed to be making money in the industry was Bill Gates. Even Gates himself speculated on the future of Microsoft in *Forbes Greatest Business Stories of All Time*, a book by Daniel Gross. Gates said, "[Microsoft] has done some good work, but all of these products become obsolete so fast . . . It will be some finite number of years, and I don't know the number—before our doom comes."

More troubling were accusations that Microsoft was using anticompetitive tactics to protect its strong market position. The sudden access to new programs on the Internet had further highlighted how incompatible Microsoft was with other competitors. Tightly "bundled" together, only Microsoft programs seemed to run properly on the Microsoft operating system. This was especially true when using network browsers to explore the World Wide Web. Microsoft's browser, dubbed Explorer, was rapidly stealing market share from Netscape, a competitor. With the launch of

Windows 98, the competition had seen enough and the lawsuits began.

In addition to complaining about the restrictive licensing deals Microsoft had with other manufacturers, which limited or outright banned alternative offerings, competitors demanded that Microsoft make it easier for users to install and run alternate programs. Ongoing lawsuits, brought by the United States, multiple states, and several foreign governments, would find that Microsoft had in fact abused its position to hinder fair competition. Perhaps at this moment, Gates was wishing he hadn't dropped out of college, especially not finishing his law degree. Under questioning he was rather elusive, which was not helping his defense. A *Business Week* article on the litigation reported Gates said, "'I don't recall' so many times that even the presiding judge had to chuckle." Despite his best efforts, Gates's and Microsoft's defense was undermined by e-mails he had sent and received that confirmed many of the charges of antitrust.

Microsoft was deemed an abusive monopoly by the courts in a judgment handed down in the case of *United States v. Microsoft* in 2000. Fines and settlements would cost the company hundreds of millions of dollars, while the European Union continues to sue

On CNN, Bill Gates reacts to a court ruling for the breakup of Microsoft Corporation on June 7, 2000. Later, it was partly overturned by the federal court.

Microsoft for anticompetitive business practices. As a result of the many lawsuits, Microsoft would be forced to rewrite its programs to allow others to be installed and run appropriately.

The stranglehold that Gates had over the computing industry was slowly ending, as was his time at Microsoft. In 2000, just after the company was called an abusive monopoly, Gates installed his college friend Steve Ballmer as CEO. Although he would remain chairman of the board, Gates said that he now wanted to focus solely on technology instead of

On January 13, 2000, Steve Ballmer *(left)* and Bill Gates announce that Ballmer will replace Gates as Microsoft CEO, with Gates remaining chairman and chief software architect.

management and strategy. Removing himself from the spotlight was a wise move. It freed him to consider new innovations and to rethink his vision, his company, and his own future.

FIVE

ICON AND IMAGE

It is impossible to know how Bill Gates has felt over the years, especially as he was being praised then attacked. His individual identity was attached to Microsoft and its many products that were now in the homes of millions of Americans. Few have attained Gates's position, but it seems that few people can bear such heated attention for long. Indeed, those attacking Gates and his company couldn't either, as proved by the "dot-com bust" in 2000, when almost all of the Internet startup companies lost their stock value and seemed to disappear overnight. Sanity had returned to the stock market, and

Microsoft had survived its greatest storm, but its leader had ceded the helm for other interests. One unanswered question remained, however: Had Microsoft's anticompetitive behavior undermined innovation in the software industry? If Microsoft didn't have such restrictive licensing deals and secretive source code, could other companies have thrived and even challenged Microsoft?

It is telling that Gates, easily considered the most important visionary of the past several decades, is actually a highly private person. Although forced into the limelight, giving speeches and demonstrations of his products, Gates appreciates his time alone with friends and family. His hobbies and interests are those of many people, like playing golf and bridge, and he spends most of his time being an active father and businessman. But his personal life, due to his success and importance, is rather exceptional. Gates's card-playing partner is billionaire investor Warren Buffett, and Gates is a collector of rare and intensely valuable artifacts such as the Codex Leicester, a collection of writings by Leonardo da Vinci, valued at more than $30 million; as well as a rare Gutenberg Bible. Everything he does draws both praise and scrutiny, even when he built his new home.

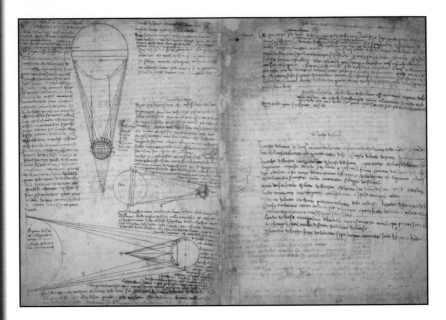

The Codex Leicester is an invaluable, seventy-two-page collection of Leonardo da Vinci's handwritten theories and thoughts on astronomy, geology, and other scientific topics.

Gates at Home

Gates's futuristic home was built to overlook Lake Washington in Medina, Washington, just outside of Seattle, near the sprawling Microsoft Redmond corporate campus. It was Gates's personal reward for his decades of diligent work, but again, it led to critical responses by the public. The large compound, reportedly among the world's most expensive homes, with an assessed value at $125 million, was purpose-fully built into the side of a hill, earth-sheltered and

Bill Gates's sprawling 37,000-square-foot home had twenty-four bathrooms, six kitchens, and only four bedrooms before his third child was born.

fully integrated with the latest technology. Gates's home where he, his wife, and three children live is actually a technological marvel. Its appliances, air conditioning, and security system are all run by software that communicates together and is completely controlled by touch screens or a single click over the Internet. It is not only a home, but a way for Gates to test new technologies and show the world the future. It includes a full movie theater and every gadget available. Some critics joked that the home would crash, like Microsoft software was prone to do, while most simply envied such a structure. Starting with personal computers, Gates has now expanded his vision to include how we live, interact, and even play.

After the dot-com bust of the late 1990s, many of Microsoft and Gates's most vicious critics came to see his wisdom. Microsoft's Office (a suite of programs, including Word, Excel, and PowerPoint) was emerging as the best-selling application in history, while the company's operating system remained the primary choice of most consumers. In fact, Microsoft's dominance remains relatively unrivaled in the technology industry. By riding out the over-exuberance of the dot-com boom, and thereby avoiding the bust, Microsoft had maintained its position and created an incredibly successful new generation of products.

A Growing Empire

Microsoft entered the multibillion-dollar computer gaming industry with its personal gaming system, Xbox. The system was a success, immediately grabbing market share away from other gaming companies such as Sony, maker of the popular

Bill Gates introduces the Xbox, Microsoft's entry into the video game market, in the Tokyo shopping district of Shibuya on February, 21, 2002.

PlayStation, which further increased Microsoft's revenues. Meanwhile, the company was releasing new versions of its networking products to serve corporations. Windows 2000 received much praise, allaying concerns about security and stability, and helping the company to gain greater market share in the highly lucrative corporate world. Once again the former allies, Microsoft and IBM, were going head-to-head, this time when trying to serve business customers. Interestingly, IBM abandoned the personal computer business altogether in 2005, selling its PC unit to Lenovo, a Chinese computer manufacturer, mostly due to the slowing growth of the PC market and IBM's refocus on corporate markets and technology services. If anything, most experts agree, IBM and Microsoft will need to work together, as they did when creating the PC in the early 1990s, to serve the critical needs of corporations in the future.

Gates, no longer CEO, was slowly improving Microsoft's products, culminating in a near-total rewrite of the operating system with the successful launch of Windows XP. His talents and focus on innovation were again paying huge dividends. Just as Gates was reinventing his products and company, so, too, was he reinventing his personal image.

The Bill and Melinda Gates Foundation

In 2000, Gates created the Bill and Melinda Gates Foundation, a charity with a focus on global education and health care. Funding college scholarships for minorities and libraries in small towns, Gates and his wife were using their wealth to help educate the masses. From 2000 to 2005, the foundation pledged a remarkable $7 billion to needy causes, including helping hundreds of community libraries. More than $3 billion was committed to global health, and more

On December 2, 1998, Bill and Melinda Gates announce a $100 million gift to establish the Bill and Melinda Gates Children's Vaccine Program during a New York press conference.

than $2 billion for educational opportunities, including bringing computers and Internet access to public libraries through the Gates Library Initiative. Additional millions were pledged to special projects across the country and in the Pacific Northwest. By 2005, the Bill and Melinda Gates Foundation had become the largest philanthropic foundation in the world, endowed with more than $29 billion.

By now Gates was enjoying life out of the public eye, in charge of Microsoft's products and doing charity work with his wife, Melinda. Over the years the harsh criticism of Gates ebbed, and a new appreciation for his work was on the rise. Multiple honorary degrees were bestowed on the college dropout, and in 2005, Queen Elizabeth II of England knighted him. He was further honored when the Gates name was used to identify a flower fly, *Eristalis gatesi*. Gates's comeback was extraordinary; after so much scrutiny, he was becoming the image of both innovation and philanthropy.

Still, Microsoft remained a target for critics and foes. Linux and other open-source applications

Melinda and Bill Gates pose outside of Buckingham Palace on March 2, 2005, shortly after Queen Elizabeth II officially knighted the technology pioneer.

continue to threaten the company's hold, as do ongoing lawsuits about its anticompetitive behavior. Microsoft's more than 90 percent share of the personal computer market remains consistent to this day, but new ideas such as Apple's iPod have shown how better and more stylish gadgets can grab the interest of the masses and create entirely new markets and revenue streams. "Stripped-down" versions of Windows for hand-held computing are growing in popularity, but as Microsoft enters new markets it encounters more competition—usually with mixed results. The Internet remains a highly competitive area, with Google and other companies battling for viewers and advertising dollars, ever reliant on the next great idea to grab the public's interest. Still, under Gates's product direction, Microsoft has continued to diversify and expand its reach, most recently into the area of robotics.

As technology has matured, so has Gates. His future has become clearer and is not focused on computers at all. In 2006, the man who started the most important computer company in the world announced that he would be leaving Microsoft in 2008. He was ending his career with the company he started not for another venture, but to help the world's most needy. The richest man on Earth decided to fully devote himself and his wealth to charity, working with his wife Melinda to make the Bill and Melinda Gates Foundation a true catalyst for change. The foundation's top priorities remain education, health care, global health issues, and global poverty. The work is challenging and expansive.

The computer industry was shocked by Gates's announcement, but the response was equally amazing. Warren Buffett, Bill Gates's friend and fellow bridge partner, announced a week later that he was giving about $50 billion of his own money to the Bill and Melinda Gates Foundation to further Gates's dream of helping the world's poorest and sickest people. Suddenly, the Gateses had more than $80 billion to help all kinds of people all around the world. Interestingly, Buffett's one requirement in donating the vast majority of his wealth was that at least one of the Gateses—Bill or Melinda—remains involved in the donating process. He insisted on a consistent vision, making it a mandate upon granting $50 billion to the foundation. Interestingly, several other wealthy businesspeople soon acted in the same manner, whether donating money to fight poverty or global warming. All it took was one to take the first step, to lead; and it was no small surprise that that person was Gates.

Warren Buffett, the second-richest person in the world, and Bill Gates play bridge on December 2, 2000, during a tournament in Omaha, Nebraska.

Understanding what his vision for computing has done over the past three decades, few can question all that Gates brought to fighting poverty and epidemics in the United States and throughout the world. Speculation still rages on about Microsoft's history, but most experts agree that the Bill and Melinda Gates Foundation, like Microsoft, will focus on innovation— vaccines and long-term solutions—to cure the world's many problems. With more than $80 billion, the foundation is well armed to tackle such a huge challenge. Under such proven leadership, the optimism is well founded.

S I X PRESENT AND FUTURE

There is much yet to be written about the life of Bill Gates. His self-created career in software was the first half; now, like his life so far, he is in charge of what comes next. Having accomplished so much in computing, there is little question why he would leave the industry, making room for other, younger people to take charge. Gates himself always knew that the business of making software was ever changing. If anything is certain, however, it's the legacy that Gates is leaving behind. Anyone who has ever used a computer owes him gratitude for his decades of work.

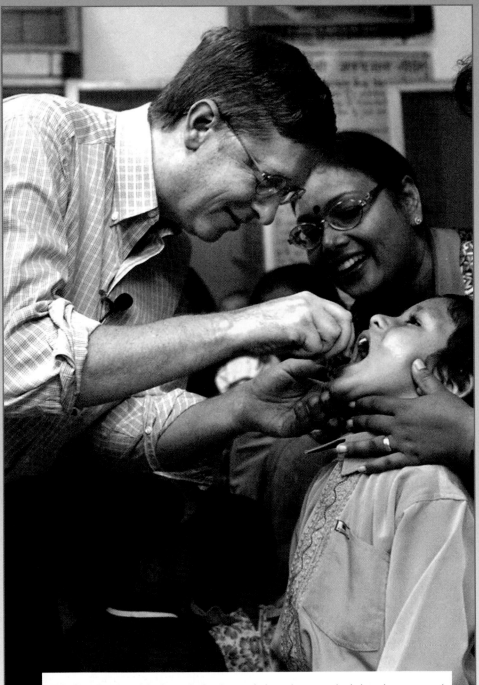

Bill Gates takes his foundation's work hands-on, administering an oral polio vaccine in New Delhi, India, on September 14, 2000.

Still, many industry experts look to Gates's decisions with a sense of loss. What technologies never became because Microsoft had such control over the entire software market? Multiple lawsuits have proven that the company—and Bill Gates— engaged in anticompetitive behavior. Was there another company that was squashed because it couldn't get licensing deals or become compatible with Windows? These are impossible questions, but they do need to be asked. Do the fines Microsoft has been forced to pay, and ongoing litigation in the European Union, make up for a truly revolu- tionary idea that never became because it didn't match Gates's vision? Nobody will ever know these answers. Future oversight over Microsoft's activities is incredibly important; the government, corporations, and citizens must continually demand fair business practices to encourage competition. Capitalism is based on competition, and when one company cheats, the whole system loses.

By now everyone knows that Microsoft's products aren't the best, but they still are the standard. Was the company's success due more to corporate malfeasance, partnering, and marketing than innova- tion? Concerning Gates specifically, most critics point to the fact that he holds nine patents, which is very few for such a highly touted innovator, especially considering that Microsoft holds thousands of patents. Gates's leadership of the company brought it to great heights, while the future of Microsoft remains to be seen without Gates's involvement. Other companies are only too eager to takes its customers and position. Hopefully, the antitrust law-suits will make the market more fair and open, with all people able to buy and benefit from the truly "best" products. Google and the iPod are the latest examples of new and truly great innovations. The future is a blank slate, for Gates and the world. With global warming and pandemics on the rise, great ideas are needed now more than ever.

Who Will Lead the Next Revolution?

What few people can argue, however, is the impact that Gates has had on industry and society. He actually made being a geek quite cool, especially since computer nerds were no longer outcasts. Savvy kids and adults who are hip to the latest technol-ogy are embraced, hired, and employed with sizeable salaries—all due to their creativity and intelligence. More important, Gates helped invent an important industry, as well as forever altered how we live, work, and play. It is safe to say that the next

Bill Gates is playing on a computer right now—maybe in America or India, Africa, or China—maybe still in elementary school, but already understanding complex technology.

Computers, and especially the Internet, concern many adults and parents, but everyone must be reminded that Gates was hacking computers before he was an American icon and the world's richest man. We must encourage innovation, but also remain wary of monopolies and terrorists using the same technology to either limit competition or cause harm.

On July 9, 2001, Bill Gates works with students in a computer lab at Booker T. Washington High School in Miami, Florida, where he has donated generous technology grants.

Computers have changed the world, and people such as Gates led their evolution. What comes next is up to another generation. Who will lead the next revolution?

Strangely enough, it may not be computers or Microsoft for which Bill Gates will be remembered. His next mission is far more important than software and gadgets. Global education and health care, addressing poverty in the developing world, and at last bringing hope to billions of needy people are far greater concerns than profits. Gates is using the profits from his past life, computing, to finance his next great

On November, 11, 2002, Bill Gates addresses a press conference in New Delhi, India, where he has given $100 million to combat the spread of HIV/AIDS.

visionary enterprise. Whatever people think of Gates as a person or businessman, no one should be against his lofty goals for helping those who need it most.

In his teens, Gates already knew what he wanted to do. By the age of twenty, he was starting a company; and at age thirty-one, he became a multi-millionaire. His vision of bringing a computer into every home has been fulfilled. Now Gates is entering his fifties a relatively youthful and healthy man with great talent, intelligence, and energy. What will he accomplish next? The Bill and Melinda Gates Foundation has already begun the fight against polio, malaria, and illiteracy. If his past is any sign, there are few things that a creative and confident person can't accomplish. With more than $80 billion to fund good causes—and maybe a little luck—there is no telling what he could accomplish.

The future has yet to be written. One can only hope that Gates is wiser from his decades in business. The antitrust activities of his company cannot be repeated with the health and welfare of so many now at stake. His focus on the Bill and Melinda Gates Foundation instead of Microsoft may allow him to change the world once more. The partner-ships that Gates forged in building Microsoft will be

In New York City, Bill Gates makes an onstage appearance for an MTV News presentation, "The Notorious BG: A Forum with Bill Gates," on October 13, 2005.

critical in the coming years. So, too, will his involvement and leadership.

Bringing education and health care to developing countries cannot include selfish aspirations; it is a team effort, building and learning together. There may never be a time when everyone is totally cured, all threats and illness abated, so Gates's dedication is paramount. He may just be the man to lead the mission to thwart global poverty and disease. Although few have dared to accept such a lofty challenge, Bill Gates has proven himself as more than capable of changing the world.

October 28, 1955 William (Bill) Henry Gates III is born in Seattle, Washington.

1967 Gates, age thirteen, enrolls in Lakeside School, where he meets Paul Allen.

1968 Gates, Allen, and two others form Lakeside Programming Group.

1973 Gates enrolls in Harvard University, where he meets Steve Ballmer.

January 1975 *Popular Electronics* features the Altair 8800 on its cover. Gates and Allen contact its manufacturer, MITS, and write a version of BASIC for the Altair.

1975 Gates and Allen form Micro-Soft; Gates drops out of Harvard and relocates to Albuquerque, New Mexico. In November, they drop the hyphen from their company name.

1979 Microsoft opens its first international office in Japan; Microsoft's headquarters move to Bellevue, Washington.

1983 Allen is diagnosed with Hodgkin's disease, resigns from Microsoft.

April 16, 1984 Gates makes his first appearance on the cover of *Time* magazine.

March 13, 1986 Microsoft goes public with its stock; Gates instantly becomes a millionaire.

January 1, 1994 Gates marries Melinda French.

November 18, 1995 Gates releases his first book, *The Road Ahead*.

January 13, 2000 Gates announces that Ballmer will replace him as CEO of Microsoft; the Bill and Melinda Gates Foundation is formed this month.

April 3, 2000 In *United States v. Microsoft*, the court rules that Microsoft is an "abusive monopoly."

March 2, 2005 Queen Elizabeth II bestows Gates with an honorary knighthood.

June 15, 2006 Microsoft announces that Gates will leave the company by July 2008 to focus on the Bill and Melinda Gates Foundation.

GLOSSARY

anti-trust Unfair and illegal activities that limit or undermine competition.

clone Version of software or hardware that may not share the same design, but serves the same functions as the original.

code The commands programmers use to create software.

copyright The official right to manufacture, produce, or sell something.

CPU The central processing unit that allows computers to operate.

GUI Graphical user interface; the way a computer, its screen, and mouse interact with the user.

hack To unlawfully access a computer; to create computer programs as a hobby.

hardware The physical components of a computer (screen, parts, adapters, etc.).

nondisclosure agreement An official agreement to keep conversations and information confidential, frequently signed when new products are shared before official release.

operating system The essential software that communicates with the CPU; other programs must be compatible with the operating system, including Windows and UNIX.

personal computer A single computer for use by a person or household, as compared to a server for a company with several users.

software The codes and programs that make computer hardware operate.

spam E-mail messages sent in large amounts to anyone, usually to scam an unknowing person or steal his or her personal and financial information.

FOR MORE INFORMATION

Association for Computing Machinery (ACM)
2 Penn Plaza, Suite 701
New York, NY 10121-0701
(800) 342-6626
Web site: http://www.acm.org

Bill and Melinda Gates Foundation
P.O. Box 23350
Seattle, WA 98102
(206) 709-3100
E-mail: info@gatesfoundation.org
Web site: http://www.gatesfoundation.org

Computer History Museum
1401 N. Shoreline Boulevard
Mountain View, CA 94043
(650) 810-1010
Web site: http://www.computerhistory.org

Computerworld
One Speen Street
Framingham, MA 01701

(508) 879-0700

Web site: http://www.computerworld.com

IEEE Computer Society

1730 Massachusetts Avenue NW

Washington, DC 20036-1992

(202) 371-0101

Web site: http://www.computer.org

Microsoft Corporation

One Microsoft Way

Redmond, WA 98052-6399

(800) MICROSOFT (642-7676)

Web site: http://www.microsoft.com

Web Sites

Due to the changing nature of Internet links, the Rosen Publishing Group, Inc., has developed an online list of Web sites related to the subject of this book. This site is updated regularly. Please use this link to access the list:

http://www.rosenlinks.com/cp/biga

FOR FURTHER READING

Baase, Sara. *A Gift of Fire: Social, Legal, and Ethical Issues in Computing.* Upper Saddle River, NJ: Prentice Hall, 2002.

Friedman, Thomas. *The World Is Flat.* New York, NY: Farrar Straus Giroux, 2005.

Gates, Bill. *Business @ the Speed of Thought.* New York, NY: Warner Books, 1999.

Gates, Bill. *The Road Ahead* New York, NY: Viking, 1995.

Gladwell, Malcolm. *The Tipping Point.* New York, NY: Little, Brown and Company, 2000.

Levitt, Steven, and Stephen Dubner. *Freakonomics: A Rogue Economist Explores the Hidden Side of Everything.* New York, NY: William Morrow, 2005.

Slater, Robert. *Microsoft Rebooted: How Bill Gates and Steve Ballmer Reinvented Their Company.* New York, NY: Penguin Group, Inc., 2004.

Wallace, James. *Hard Drive: Bill Gates and the Making of the Microsoft Empire.* New York, NY: Harper Business, 1993.

Wozniak, Steve. *From Computer Geek to Cult Icon: How I Invented the Personal Computer,*

Co-Founded Apple, and Had Fun Doing It. New York, NY: W.W. Norton, 2006.

Wukovits, John. *Bill Gates: Software King*. London, England: Franklin Watts, 2000.

BIBLIOGRAPHY

Baldauf, Scott. "Bill Gates, the Biggest Thing in India Since the Beatles." *Christian Science Monitor* online. November 14, 2002. Retrieved October 16, 2006 (http://www.csmonitor.com/2002/1114/p07s02-wosc.html).

Bank, David. "Breaking Windows." *Wall Street Journal* online. February 19, 1999. Retrieved May 16, 2006 (http://www.breakingwindows.net/1link3.htm).

Chposky, James, and Ted Leonsis. *Blue Magic: The People, the Power and the Politics Behind the IBM Personal Computer.* New York, NY: Facts on File, Inc., 1989.

Fried, Ina. "Gates Joins Board of Buffett's Berkshire Hathaway." CNET News. December 14, 2004. Retrieved October 16, 2006 (http://news.com.com/Gates+joins+board+of+Buffetts+Berkshire+Hathaway/2100-1014_3-5491312.html).

Gates, Bill. *Business @ the Speed of Thought.* New York, NY: Warner Books, 1999.

Gates, Bill. *The Road Ahead.* New York, NY: Viking, 1995.

"Gates Deposition Makes Judge Laugh in Court."
CNN. November 17, 1998. Retrieved October 16,
2006 (http://www.cnn.com/TECH/computing/
9811/17/judgelaugh.ms.idg/index.html).

"The Gates Operating System." *Time*. January 13,
1997. Retrieved May 16, 2005.

Lammers, Susan. *Programmers at Work*. Redmond,
WA: Microsoft Press, 1986.

Manes, Stephen, and Paul Andrews. *Gates: How
Microsoft's Mogul Reinvented an Industry and
Made Himself the Richest Man in America*. New
York, NY: Touchstone, 1993.

"Microsoft Announces Plans for July 2008 Transition
for Bill Gates." Microsoft PressPass. June 15, 2006.
Retrieved October 16, 2006 (http://www.microsoft.
com/presspass/press/2006/jun06/
06-15CorpNewsPR.mspx).

"Microsoft's Teflon Bill." *Business Week*. November 30,
1998. Retrieved October 16, 2006 (http://
www.businessweek.com/1998/48/
b3606125.htm).

NPR. "Buffett Gift Sends $31 Billion to Gates
Foundation." *All Things Considered*. June 26, 2006.

Reimer, Jeremy. "Total Share: 30 Years of Personal
Computer Market Share Figures." Arstechnica.
com. December 14, 2005. Retrieved October 16,

2006 (http://arstechnica.com/articles/culture/total-share.ars/1).

Taylor III, Alexander L. "The Wizard Inside the Machine," *Time*. April 16, 1984. Retrieved December 29, 2006 (http://205.188.238.109/time/magazine/article/0,9171,954266,00.html).

INDEX

About the Author

Brad Lockwood is an award-winning author of fiction and nonfiction books, as well as magazine articles and films. A former "dot-com geek" who left the computer industry to write, he is an enthusiast of technology. Lockwood is the father of one and lives in Brooklyn, New York.

Photo Credits

Cover © Justin Sullivan/Getty Images; pp. 5, 17, 39 Courtesy Microsoft Corporation; p. 7 © Tim Crosby/Liaison Agency/Getty Images; p. 12 © Bettmann/Corbis; p. 14 Courtesy of the Jane Carlson Williams '60 Archives at Lakeside School; pp. 21, 27, 33, 44 © Ron Wurzer/Getty Images; p. 24 © Ralph Morse/Time Life Pictures/Getty Images; p. 42 © IBM/epa/Corbis; p. 46 © Time Inc./ Time Life Pictures/Getty Images; pp. 50, 54 © Deborah Feingold/ Corbis; p. 52 © Cindy Charles/Liaison/Getty Images; p. 59 © Torsten Blackwood/AFP/Getty Images; p. 61 © Gerald French/Corbis; pp. 64, 88 © AP/Wide World Photos; p. 68 © Jon Levy/AFP/Getty Images; pp. 70, 90 © Jeff Christensen/Getty Images; p. 73 © CNN/ AFP/Getty Images; p. 74 © Dan Levine/AFP/Getty Images; p. 78 Art Resource, NY; p. 79 © Dan Callister/Newsmakers/Getty Images; p. 81 © Toru Yamanaka/AFP/Getty Images; p. 83 © Timothy A. Clary/AFP/Getty Images; p. 85 © Peter Macdiarmid/Getty Images; p. 93 © Jeff Christensen/Getty Images; p. 94 © Prakash Singh/ AFP/Getty Images; p. 96 © Scott Gries/Getty Images.

Designer: Tahara Anderson; Editor: Roman Espejo;
Photo Researcher: Amy Feinberg